Music for Monoliths

Tanka by Miriam Sagan

you'll always notice
the lone tree
something that speaks
to your hidden
solitude

red bird flash
I retrieve the word
"cardinal"
I think it was redder
before I named it

I lie in bed
as pink roses explode
from bud to bloom and
the scent of lilacs fades
in dusty rain

at night moths seem
drawn by a light we cannot see
end up brittle, dead
on the bathroom floor
wisps of morning dreams

all the water
pressed from tofu
by the
collected works
of William Shakespeare

the oncologist
is on the phone but I don't
pick up or stop
dancing as Patti Smith sings
"Gimme Shelter"

source of the river
a girl spinning, the traveler
realizes he's sailed
across the Milky Way, is
himself a wandering star

swimming at night
we neglect
to visit
the observatory
that discovered Pluto

we tried to be
quiet making love
in the little inn
where the peacock
cried out so raucously

under my pillow
not a tooth for the fairy
but an elm seed
that grows like a beanstalk
into dreams above the clouds

things I didn't
pick up at the tideline:
tentacles, sea foam,
broken shell, sandpiper tracks,
my most familiar fears

musician in black
carries her violin case
on her back
through the rose garden
towards opening notes

outside
the concert hall
blue phlox flowers
rolling notes of Philip Glass
float out

double bass player—
who will love her?
who is tall enough?
whose strings
will she pluck?

tsunami warning
and a plan we half enjoy
worrying about—
marimbas of raindrops
on giant leaves

cactus wren pecks
hole in the saguaro
I admire a nest
in thorns—but am too shy
to answer your question

cloud mimics mountain
art deco dam towers
over the outflow—
something we haven't seen
has eaten this prickly pear

autumn leaves
an ordinary house
how can my story
begin until I close
this door behind me?

my husband harvests
the orchard's
Asian apple pears—
across the wall the neighbor
says: I'm glad you're not a bear

for the first time
I won't bring geraniums
in from the frost
not the pink ones
nor the red

looking at the geese
across the sky of the
Japanese print
my father shakily asks me
why the next page is blank

princess leaps
from an earthen wall—
white grasses wave
all the way to the frontier
and I don't long for home

long view
red buttes and blue mesas
in the courtyard
my own private
tumbleweed

where was I going
train under a full moon?
washing my hair
in the women's room
of the San Jose station

I don't think
it was my tears
that obscured
the ferry schedule—
just mist

music of the high
plateau
she taps the cello
as if it was
a shaman's hand drum

it's snowing inside
the house as it does
every early spring
the soprano sings that love
is coming, she is waiting

desert river flows
one-person shelter of sticks
frames the view
small waterfall, but my thoughts
flow away downstream

Ganesh sells earrings
in the jewelry store window
the poet
works at Starbuck's now
for better pay

auguries of birds
write across the sky's blank page
endlessness arrives
tells us something forgotten
that we already know

Rothko chapel
black shapes seem to rise
into air
like monoliths
of smoke

the sisters
ran from a great bear
up the butte top
fled skyward, arms outstretched
became the Pleiades

daytime moon waxing
over Devils Tower
monolith
of hexagonal crystals
as wasps buzz on the screen

look! everyone points
up where
climbers hang from rock
I won't admit it but
I'm happier on the ground

dozens of vultures
resting in pine trees
at dusk
sunset illuminates
the tower with last daylight

Devils Tower
in the rearview mirror
in the end
I choose to go
back home

pale birch driftwood
tent worms blown lakeward
everything everywhere
tossed
towards the rising water

in the hot spring
beneath white pampas grass
a woman is talking
about the dark
of the moon

icicles drip
melt, reform, glitter
the surgical scar
looks just the same as it did
this morning

there's still kale
in the winter bed—
breast lump,
knitting needles click
scarf's first inch

we stayed so late
talking
it snowed towards midnight
and your footprints heading home
filled

snow-capped volcano
the spirits of winter
sit around
the heated table
playing dice

Chinatown
restaurant like any other
I order
carefully off the menu
as if you might still appear

red monolith
some call a power vortex
but I'm just looking
for a nice place
to have lunch

recite talismans
of other destinations
of elsewhere, where
you will go once you finish
reading this book

half life
of uranium
older than mountains—
radiation for the
miner's lung cancer

the toddler's fit
not this spoon, that spoon
not that blanket
the other one—then lulled
to cherubic sleep

pelicans
scour the shrimp boat
a weekday
fisherman casts his lines
from the pier

waiting for you
I turn the pages
of a novel
where a woman goes mad
waiting

low tide
a wooden boat sunk
in mud flats
I also am
going nowhere

old tanka poet
dies—I'm embarrassed
by the details
of his illness—
just want his words

Camel Rock
has lost its nose—
in the casino
gamblers press buttons
in a haze of hope

marigolds
in the heat—
do I really want
to know how much time
I have left?

trash in the tree
housefly at the window
I sit
by the old woman dying—
spring wind

old letters
and diaries…the wind
has archived
tumbleweed
against the barbed wire fence

birdsong in mist
an old tale of revenge,
in the birch forest
even the greatest archer
can't hit the moon

distance between
sea and mountains
sleep and waking
me and you, you and me
so close so far

and on our return
the pink rosebush had gone wild
almost blocked the door
we weren't gone that long
but it rained in the desert

Jizo statue
wrapped in string, each cord
a lost object
I will not find
again

Notes on the Tanka

"at night moths" is based on "Canzona di Ringraziamento" for flute, by Salvatore Sciarrino, 1985.

"outside" is based on Symphony No. 14 by Philip Glass, American premier at Spoleto Festival USA, South Carolina, 2023.

"music of the high" is based on "Tibetan Dance" for solo cello by Bright Sheng.

"it's snowing inside" is based on the opera "Vanessa" by Samuel Barber.

"desert river flows" is based on an eco-arts installation by Basia Irland, Santa Fe, New Mexico, USA, 2023.

"auguries of birds" is based on the painting "Auguries" by Julie Mehretu in the Denver Art Museum.

Devils Tower is part of an ancient volcanic formation in Wyoming, USA. It is a national monument, also known as Bear Lodge Butte. And it is sacred to several Native American tribes.

"distance between" is based on "Distance" by Jonah Gallagher, as performed by the Del Sol Quartet.

Afterward

My relationship to Japanese poetic forms, in their American incarnation, has been lifelong. I began writing haiku—or what passed for it—in grade school. As a young poet and graduate student in creative writing I focused on contemporary free verse, a form I have spent my life following. Some writers find the two paths antithetical and don't practice both haiku and contemporary poetry in English. However, many of the Japanese-based forms—haiku, senryu, haibun, and renga—have held my enduring interest.

In 1984, I moved to Santa Fe, NM, from San Francisco. I sent a change of address to the editor of *Frogpond,* where I was publishing regularly. A note came back from Elizabeth Searle Lamb saying we were about to become neighbors, and inviting me to tea. She became one of my dearest friends until her death in 2005. Despite our proximity, we corresponded by mail and wrote renga in that medium, later supplanted by email. Lamb was a modernist and didn't rigidly adhere to rules. After her death, I helped her daughter Carolyn Lamb clean out Elizabeth's casita on the Acequia Madre, an ancient irrigation ditch that gave her street its name. Elizabeth left haiku everywhere: on slips of paper, bedside, on the kitchen table, tucked into sofa cushions. As a way to continue our conversations I started writing haiku in response to her unpublished ones. This became the chapbook *Dream That Is Not A Dream* (Miriam's Well).

I then began to focus mostly on writing tanka. I enjoyed the longer form which emphasized the lyrical and the personal. I published *Tanka from The Edge* (Modern English Tanka) and was glad to have so many tanka collected. Then it was back to haiku, and recently tanka again. It is not that I can only write one or the other at any given time, rather than parts of my inner life seem to evoke either haiku or tanka. How fortunate I am to have followed this path. My approach is to write an "American" version of the forms, reflecting my own language and culture. I'm indebted to the traditional forms, and delighted at how they have spread worldwide, uniting people who want to pursue their craft.

This collection was started some time ago when I wrote several dreamy tanka that evoked archetypes and fairy tales. A recent health crisis put me more deeply in touch with illness and mortality. And then there were the tanka of daily life, of travel and landscape, of householding and family. Could these go together? I suspected they could but had to print them and then cut them out with a big scissors. I spread the poems on my bed in an attempt to assemble a whole.

Then I had some additional ideas. Monoliths—large free-standing geologic features—appeared in the tanka but not prominently. Could this be expanded? I'd always wanted to visit Devils Tower, a national monument, in Wyoming. A more appropriate name for the site might be Bear Lodge, reflecting the Native American view and having no negative spiritual connotations. It took two days to drive there, but the experience surpassed my expectations. My tanka pilgrimage yielded what I needed.

Large rocks always seem to be humming to me. I wanted to capture some of this music of the earth. I also always carry a tiny notebook and have found myself scribbling when listening to live music. Numerous musical compositions and some visual art are the direct inspiration for a variety of tanka. The Notes list these sources with my gratitude.

There is that pleasing and reassuring moment when a book comes together, when I realize that indeed my sensibility is consistent even as circumstances change. Each of these tanka was a gift to me and I hope to the reader as well. Please enjoy.

Many of these tanka first appeared in *Atlas Poetica.*